Stringstorm

Level 9 – Gold

Helpful Hints for Reading at Home

The graphemes (written letters) and phonemes (units of sound) used throughout this series are aligned with Letters and Sounds. This offers a consistent approach to learning whether reading at home or in the classroom.

HERE ARE SOME COMMON WORDS THAT YOUR CHILD MIGHT FIND TRICKY:

water	where	would	know	thought	through	couldn't
laughed	eyes	once	we're	school	can't	our

TOP TIPS FOR HELPING YOUR CHILD TO READ:

- Encourage your child to read aloud as well as silently to themselves.
- Allow your child time to absorb the text and make comments.
- Ask simple questions about the text to assess understanding.
- Encourage your child to clarify the meaning of new vocabulary.

This book focuses on developing independence, fluency and comprehension. It is a gold level 9 book band.

OXFORDSHIRE COUNTY COUNCIL	
3303744438	
Askews & Holts	13-Sep-2022
JF BEGINNER READER	

Stringstorm

Written by
Hermione Redshaw

Illustrated by
Marianne Constable

Bertie hated water.

He did not like swimming and refused to go paddling. He would not touch the washing up, and if being clean was not so important, he would never take a bath.

Bertie had ways of avoiding these things and he had mastered the art of speed-bathing.

Only one thing managed to sneak up on him: rain. He could be carrying an umbrella around for nothing, but if he forgot his coat one day, he may as well have gone swimming.

Even one drop of the stuff was too much for Bertie.

Fortunately, Bertie was inventing a way to put a stop to rain altogether.

It helped, of course, that Bertie was a genius inventor. He created all sorts of things around the house that made his life easier – from automatic egg crackers to a machine that made broccoli taste like chocolate – but never anything on this scale.

Bertie needed to test his new invention first, and the shower was the closest he could get to rain.

Great success! Every last drop of water that fell from the shower head was string.

There was a slight mishap when Bertie was examining it. Mum unplugged the machine for the vacuum and the water falling became water again!

"I can't be having that happen!" thought a sodden Bertie.

Mum rushed to his aid with a towel. She even found a pair of scissors to clean up the mess of soggy string in the bathtub. However, Bertie was still unhappy.

"My great invention, foiled by unplugging? The machine needs to run on its own."

It took a measly 21 updates to get the machine perfect enough for Bertie. After lots of research, he had finally mastered it. THE STRING MASTER MK.22! Now, the only thing left to do was test it.

Dad offered to help take the String Master Mk.22 up to the roof – a kind offer, but Bertie knew what was coming. Once they got there and the machine was set up, Dad would not leave. He said he was "supervising," but he kept asking questions.

"What've you made, son?" or, "Do you need a hand, Bertie?" and finally, when Bertie had been staring up at the sky for about 20 minutes, "What are you waiting for?"

"The rain," Bertie replied irritably.

Dad frowned and scratched his head. He knew how much Bertie hated the rain, so why was he waiting for it?

A drop of rain hit Bertie's nose. Hastily, he fired up the String Master Mk.22. The next drop was not water at all. It was string! It worked! The clouds turned from wisps to wool, pouring string across the rooftop.

"Wow!" uttered Dad. "Is everywhere raining string?"
"Only our rooftop, for now," said Bertie. "But if I turn this dial…"

However, when Bertie turned the dial, rain splattered his head. Downstairs, Mum had unplugged the machine again, this time to yell, "Dinner's ready!"
"I thought I'd fixed that," grumbled Bertie.

The problem was that he did not remember. He HAD fixed it. That evening, as Bertie ate, the machine whirred back to life.

When Bertie went to sleep that night, his worries that the machine might be broken were forgotten. Instead, he dreamt about the mayor offering him a prize and lots of money for the String Master. Then, he started to ponder what his next successful invention might be.

The next morning, Bertie stumbled out of bed and got ready to go to school as normal. However, there were quite a few strange things that happened. First, the taps would not work. No matter which taps Bertie tried, he still had to brush his teeth with a bottle of sparkling water.

Next, the TV would not work. Fortunately, the Wi-Fi did. Dad put the local news stream on while Bertie ate his cereal.

"Schools are closed today," said the news reporter.
"Closed?" echoed Mum, while Bertie whooped and cheered. "What for?"
"Maybe for the snow," said Dad, pointing to the window.
"Snow?" said Mum. "In June?"

Everyone from the building piled out into the street. Though the ground was blanketed in something fluffy, it was not snow – it was string!

Layers upon layers of fluffy threads covered the streets. Vehicles could not move far. The string wrapped around wheels, dragging all traffic to a halt.

"Bertie?" Dad said, in that stern voice parents used when you were in trouble.
"The machine was off, I'm sure it was!" said Bertie. "Look – it's not raining string now!"

Dad decided to believe him.

"I can't get to work now!" he said.
"Nothing scissors wouldn't solve," said Mum.

Dad sighed. He would have enjoyed a day off.

Bertie spent his day off school watching TV and thinking up new inventions to make money. Of course, he had not won any prizes for the String Master yet. No one knew he had made it, so how would they know where to call?

However, when the weather programme started, Bertie's dreams of gold faded.

A rainstorm was forecast for tonight! Bertie swallowed a lump in his throat. He told Mum and Dad the machine was off, but he had not checked that was true – Dad would not let him.

"There are terrible winds outside," Dad had said. "Maybe tomorrow."

When Bertie woke up the following day, he was excited to see that Mum and Dad were still in pyjamas.

"Another day of no school?" he asked.

Mum and Dad did not respond. They were staring at the TV, their mouths open.

The news reporter was stood outside with string up to her waist. Even more flew at her face.

"The stringstorm has arrived in full force! People are stuck in their homes with string blocking their doors. Roads are closed due to string walls between lamp posts. We're not sure where it came from, but if anyone can help–"

A large ball of string bowled her over.

Mum and Dad looked to Bertie, but he was already gone. He raced up the stairs to the roof. String flew at his face in gales, and up here, where it all started, the string on the ground was almost as tall as him. He could not see where the String Master was amongst it all.

"Where did I put it?" Bertie muttered desperately.

Then, a tap on his shoulder made him jump. Mum and Dad had followed him to the roof. "We came to help!" Dad said.

They were both holding pairs of scissors. They even had a pair for Bertie. So, the three of them set to work cutting through the string.

Finally, Bertie uncovered the String Master Mk.22, whirring away aggressively. Bertie looked for the off switch, but of course, he had not installed one! The plug was already unplugged and he had not thought about ever needing to turn off one of his inventions.

"I don't know what to do," said Bertie, horrified. He had tried every button, dial and switch. He even tried kicking it. "I can't stop it!"

Then, Mum swooped in, armed with nothing but her pair of scissors, and the machine suddenly stopped.

The clouds overhead turned back to normal and the string settled on the ground as rain began to fall in its place. Bertie had never been so happy to feel rain.

The rain washed away most of the string on the roof and across the city. People were finally free from their homes and flocked to the streets, cheering for the rain.

Bertie still had a big job to do to help clean up what string was left, but for the first time, he was thankful for the rain.

"This wind is a pain, though," said Bertie, thinking of a new invention.

"Bertie, NO!" said Mum and Dad.

Stringstorm

1. What does Bertie hate?

    a) String

    b) His hair

    c) Water

2. What is an invention?

3. What was Bertie's big invention called?

4. How do you think Bertie felt when he couldn't turn off his machine?

5. Can you come up with a new invention to make life better or easier?

©2022 **BookLife Publishing Ltd.**
King's Lynn, Norfolk, PE30 4LS, UK

ISBN 978-1-80155-804-4

All rights reserved. Printed in Poland.
A catalogue record for this book is available from the British Library.

Stringstorm
Written by Hermione Redshaw
Illustrated by Marianne Constable

An Introduction to BookLife Readers...

Our Readers have been specifically created in line with the London Institute of Education's approach to book banding and are phonetically decodable and ordered to support each phase of Letters and Sounds.

Each book has been created to provide the best possible reading and learning experience. Our aim is to share our love of books with children, providing both emerging readers and prolific page-turners with beautiful books that are guaranteed to provoke interest and learning, regardless of ability.

BOOK BAND GRADED using the Institute of Education's approach to levelling.

PHONETICALLY DECODABLE supporting each phase of Letters and Sounds.

EXERCISES AND QUESTIONS to offer reinforcement and to ascertain comprehension.

BEAUTIFULLY ILLUSTRATED to inspire and provoke engagement, providing a variety of styles for the reader to enjoy whilst reading through the series.

AUTHOR INSIGHT:
HERMIONE REDSHAW

Hermione Redshaw has been writing books for over eight years, with a passion for adventure and fantasy. Her writing is often distinguished by themes of family and personal growth. Hermione holds a Bachelor's degree in English Language, Communication and Linguistics, with a keen interest in communicating difficult ideas in a clear and accessible way. Her Master's in Children's Publishing focused Hermione's experiments with bold and innovative concepts, from story apps to dyslexia-friendly and educational adventures. She joins BookLife Publishing with a drive to engage new and old readers alike.

This book focuses on developing independence, fluency and comprehension. It is a gold level 9 book band.